THE IMPOSTOR'S GUIDE TO AMONG US

Published in 2021 by Mortimer Children's Books Limited,
part of Welbeck Publishing Group Limited
20 Mortimer Street, London W1T 3JW

Text and design © Welbeck Children's Limited,
part of Welbeck Publishing Group Limited

The publishers would like to thank the following sources for their kind permission to reproduce the pictures in this book:

bodnar.photo/Shutterstock.com

Every effort has been made to acknowledge correctly and contact the source and/or copyright holder of each picture, any unintentional errors or omissions will be corrected in future editions of this book.

All game information correct as of November 2020.

A CIP catalogue record for this book is available from the British Library.

ISBN: 978 1 83935 083 2
Printed in Spain

1 3 5 7 9 10 8 6 4 2

Author: Kevin Pettman
Design: Rockjaw Creative
Design Manager: Matt Drew
Editorial Manager: Joff Brown
Production: Rachel Burgess

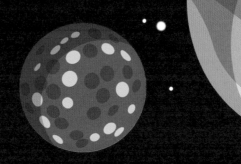

THE IMPOSTOR'S GUIDE TO AMONG US

KEVIN PETTMAN

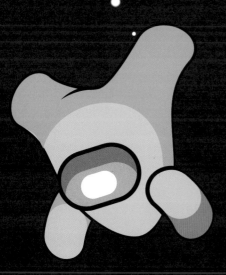

MORTIMER

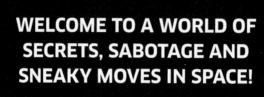

WELCOME TO A WORLD OF SECRETS, SABOTAGE AND SNEAKY MOVES IN SPACE!

Among Us is an action-packed mobile and PC game full of thrilling fun. Can you be a clever Crewmate and an ingenious Impostor? Or perhaps you're totally new to this adventure? Well don't sweat your spacesuit, because this complete guide reveals all you need to know to master the mystery and mayhem onboard your ship!

CONTENTS

OUT OF THIS WORLD...

In Among Us, you are either a Crewmate or an Impostor on a spaceship and the game strategy is simple. The Crew's job is to work together and complete tasks until the task bar is full, or track down and vote off the hidden Impostor to get a win. Watch out, because the Impostor will try to sabotage the spaceship and get victory by killing off all of the Crew, or getting innocent Crewmates ejected from the ship.

Among Us is a game of teamwork and betrayal.
Players are either Crewmates or an Impostor.

SECRET STUFF

However, the gameplay is not that simple! The tension rises as there can be as many as three Impostors in a game of ten players, which makes dashing around the maps quite crazy and dangerous. Plus, you can't choose your role, and you're only told whether you are a Crewmate or Impostor seconds before the start.

Practice in Freeplay mode!

Set your own tasks as a Crew member or practice your Impostor killing strategies!

SPACED OUT

Crewmates must act as a team to uncover the evil Impostor, but communicating is only possible in meetings. These happen after a dead body is reported or when an emergency meeting is called. The Crew can then chat, through text, and vote to say who they each think the cruel culprit is... but remember the Impostor will try to behave normal and act innocent. It's a tricky test of your detective skills!

Sabotage the ship and confuse the Crew.

Close doors and trap victims.

Kill off the Crew between cooldowns.

CREWMATES vs IMPOSTOR

How do you spot the Impostor? Well, you can't just by looking, because they appear just the same as the rest of the Crew! All players have their name above them and are identified by a suit colour. These include red, black, brown, green, yellow and white.

HAT AND SKIN COSMETICS CAN BE ADDED FOR FREE OR AS A PAID OPTION. ▶▶▶

Remove All Ads

PETS

Brainslug Pet Bundle

£2.79

DISCUSS!

WE NEED TO TALK

When someone reports a dead body or calls an emergency meeting, the Crew gathers to discuss what they know about the Impostor. Players can now talk openly about who they think the Impostor is and what information they have. When playing in person, Ghosts cannot talk as they already know who the Impostor is. Impostors will try to prove their innocence or accuse another crew member.

Blend in with the Crew.

Sneak through vents.

Pretend to run tasks.

DEADLY DETECTION

To the eye, the two types of player are no different, so dig deeper to detect the wrongdoer. The Impostor could give their identity away by strange behaviour, not taking part in tasks or being spotted faking tasks. Using vents is a dead giveaway for an Impostor, because only they are able to do that. Being the Impostor can be tense and needs lots of practice to perfect it.

JOIN THE CREW

Crewmates have safety in numbers and will often stick together, even though there is the risk of unwittingly joining up with the Impostor. The Crew looks after each other as they won't win without teamwork, but be prepared for others turning against you and suggesting you're evil... the Impostor will be sneaky and have others destroyed or ejected.

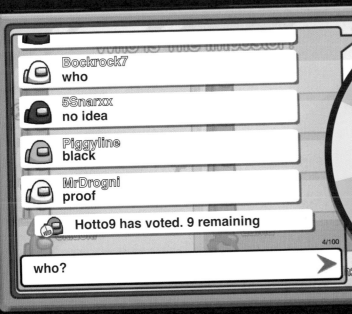

Bockrock7
who

5Snarxx
no idea

Piggyline
black

MrDrogni
proof

Hotto9 has voted. 9 remaining

4/100

who?

GRUESOME GHOST

If you're killed or ejected, or ejected as an Impostor and there are other Impostors still active, you carry on as a ghost. Ghosts are only visible to other ghosts and can move through walls.

RupertStew

9

NUMBERS TO KNOW

Time to figure out some important stats and numbers...

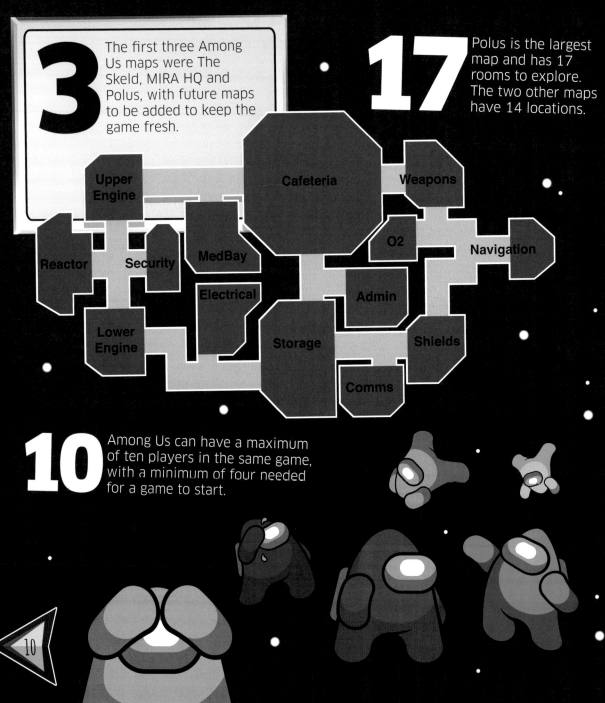

3 The first three Among Us maps were The Skeld, MIRA HQ and Polus, with future maps to be added to keep the game fresh.

17 Polus is the largest map and has 17 rooms to explore. The two other maps have 14 locations.

Upper Engine

Cafeteria

Weapons

Reactor   Security   MedBay

O2

Navigation

Electrical

Admin

Lower Engine

Storage

Shields

Comms

10 Among Us can have a maximum of ten players in the same game, with a minimum of four needed for a game to start.

60

Kill cooldown can be set as high as 60 seconds or as low as ten. It's the time the Impostor must wait to strike again after making a kill.

DEAD BODY REPORTED

100,000,000

The game has had more than 100 million downloads. On average, about 60 million gamers are thought to play each day.

impostor

HOST

Create Game

Available Games

6

A six-letter code can be shared with friends by a game host so that you can play together in the same match.

2018

Among Us was released by its developer, InnerSloth, in 2018. It wasn't until 2020 when the game became a smash hit around the world!

3

Games are allowed to have up to three Impostors, but it's more common for one or two to be included in a match.

DETECTION MANUAL

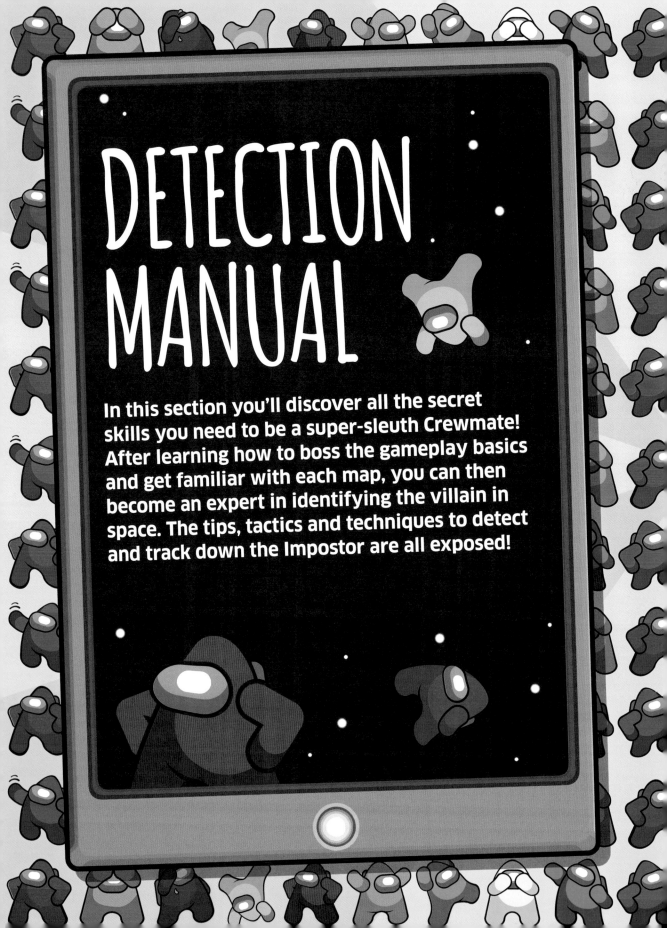

In this section you'll discover all the secret skills you need to be a super-sleuth Crewmate! After learning how to boss the gameplay basics and get familiar with each map, you can then become an expert in identifying the villain in space. The tips, tactics and techniques to detect and track down the Impostor are all exposed!

BEGIN THE BATTLE

Join the adventure as a Crewmate, know how to control a game and keep a step ahead of the Impostor.

FREEPLAY FUN

Among Us has no combat or fighting, but it's still a full-on battle to beat the bad guy! Gaining experience in how to defeat the Impostor only comes with playing and racking up game time. For newcomers, the best place to start is in Freeplay mode. From the main menu, select 'Freeplay' and choose which map to explore.

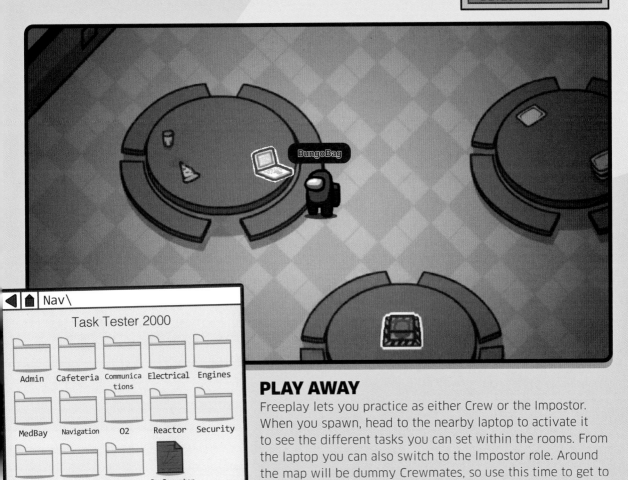

BungoBag

Nav\

Task Tester 2000

Admin	Cafeteria	Communica tions	Electrical	Engines
MedBay	Navigation	O2	Reactor	Security
Shields	Storage	Weapons	Be_Impostor .exe	

PLAY AWAY

Freeplay lets you practice as either Crew or the Impostor. When you spawn, head to the nearby laptop to activate it to see the different tasks you can set within the rooms. From the laptop you can also switch to the Impostor role. Around the map will be dummy Crewmates, so use this time to get to know the map, how to move and how to complete your tasks.

MAP MAYHEM

Each map may seem chaotic at first. Click on the map icon and all the rooms are displayed on screen. The rooms with exclamation marks show there's a task to be done there. Your current location is identified by where your avatar appears. Head to the areas which need tasks doing first and practise completing the task. There's no time limit or Impostor chasing you, so use the time to work out how to do each task – this will be a big bonus for when you're doing tasks under pressure in a real game!

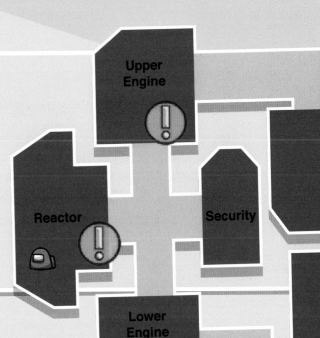

Upper Engine

Reactor

Security

Lower Engine

SELECT SETTINGS

I want to play the game **my way!**

Before a game, make sure you understand the important Among Us settings and how they affect you.

COOL CUSTOMIZATION

The type of game you create will not only depend on your role, your chosen map and whether you're a pro or a noob. There are lots of settings that will create a particular vibe and feel to a mission. If you are the game host, you can decide the settings through the 'customize' and 'game' options. The player speed, discussion time, kill distance, visible task bar, confirm ejects and emergency cooldown time are just some of the levels that can be adjusted – there are at least 12 settings to play with.

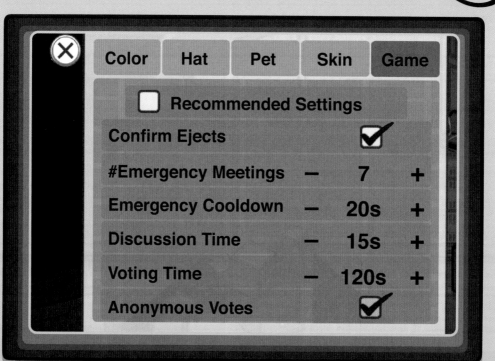

| Color | Hat | Pet | Skin | Game |

Recommended Settings

Confirm Ejects	✓
#Emergency Meetings	— 7 +
Emergency Cooldown	— 20s +
Discussion Time	— 15s +
Voting Time	— 120s +
Anonymous Votes	✓

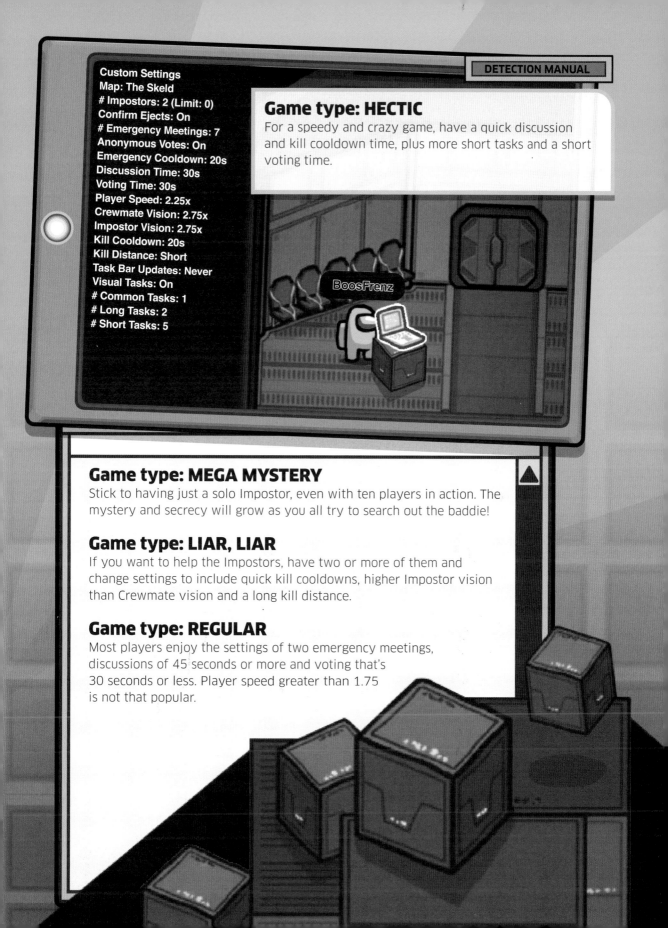

Custom Settings
Map: The Skeld
Impostors: 2 (Limit: 0)
Confirm Ejects: On
Emergency Meetings: 7
Anonymous Votes: On
Emergency Cooldown: 20s
Discussion Time: 30s
Voting Time: 30s
Player Speed: 2.25x
Crewmate Vision: 2.75x
Impostor Vision: 2.75x
Kill Cooldown: 20s
Kill Distance: Short
Task Bar Updates: Never
Visual Tasks: On
Common Tasks: 1
Long Tasks: 2
Short Tasks: 5

Game type: HECTIC

For a speedy and crazy game, have a quick discussion and kill cooldown time, plus more short tasks and a short voting time.

BoosFrenz

Game type: MEGA MYSTERY

Stick to having just a solo Impostor, even with ten players in action. The mystery and secrecy will grow as you all try to search out the baddie!

Game type: LIAR, LIAR

If you want to help the Impostors, have two or more of them and change settings to include quick kill cooldowns, higher Impostor vision than Crewmate vision and a long kill distance.

Game type: REGULAR

Most players enjoy the settings of two emergency meetings, discussions of 45 seconds or more and voting that's 30 seconds or less. Player speed greater than 1.75 is not that popular.

MAPS: THE SKELD

Take a trip around the most popular Among Us map and learn these valuable ship-based facts.

Don't get lost around this big map – move in a clockwise or anti-clockwise path to help you remember where you are.

Upper Engine

MedBay

Reactor

Security

Electrical

Lower Engine

Storag

Easy-to-use four-camera system in Security room for tracking down Impostors.

18

Crewmates in The Skeld are often at beginner or mid-level experience, with high-level players preferring MIRA HQ and Polus.

The Skeld is popular because it's the original map from the game's beginnings in 2018.

The emergency meeting button is on the Cafeteria table. Hit this if you want to gather your Crewmates for an important chat!

Weapons

The Skeld has 14 vents, so as a Crewmate be aware that Impostors may disappear and appear at the blink of an eye!

Cafeteria

O2

Navigation

Admin

COLOUR CHAOS

The map in Admin does not show the colour of players, so you won't know who specific avatars are.

Shields

Communications

The Admin room has an interactive map showing where all the game's players are, which is a helpful Crewmate tool!

19

MAPS: MIRA HQ

Head to company headquarters for a big test of your problem and puzzle-solving skills. Here, Crewmates must still keep an eye on the Impostor.

MIRA HQ is smaller and it can be tricky for the Crew to escape the evil intentions of the Impostor.

Reactor

Vents are ultra important to the Impostor in MIRA HQ. They are all connected and used a lot, so Crewmates must work together to spot their use.

Fewer hallways for Crewmates to navigate their way around, with a lot of the action inside rooms.

Entering the Decontamination area locks both doors for a short while, which may split you from your Crewmates – watch out!

Decontamination

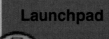

Launchpad

Greenhouse

Office

Admin

Laboratory

In the Communications room, use the door log to see a player's movements – it can help a Crewmate spot if a player has vented between locations!

Unlike The Skeld and Polus, there are no cameras to help Crewmates around this headquarters map.

MIRA HQ copies The Skeld and has the emergency meeting button in the Cafeteria. Don't forget this when you're dashing to chat with your Crew.

Locker Room

Communications

Storage

Cafeteria

MedBay

Balcony

MAPS: POLUS

Get to know this frantic and freezing location, where the Crew can face Impostor threats at any time.

Dropship

In Security there are six cameras, so Crewmates can see a lot... however only one camera is visible at a time.

Try to avoid Polus if you have less than eight players. It's too big and difficult for a limited Crew to capture the Impostor!

Electrical

Specimen and Dropship are unique rooms in Polus. Players spawn in Dropship.

Security

The southern areas of Polus, around Specimen, Admin and O2, have no vents and can be safer ground for Crewmates compared to the north.

O2

Communications

Weapons

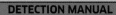

VITAL SIGNS

In the Office, open the Vitals kiosk to see which Crewmates are alive. A signal means a player is still in action.

Laboratory

Storage

The Decontamination chamber is quite big, so crewmates should avoid entering alone as the Impostor may strike while there are no witnesses to the crime!

Office

Admin

Vast outdoor areas in freezing Arctic-like conditions. There's a lot of space for Crew to get lost and attacked in!

Specimen Room

TAKE A TASK

It's essential that Crewmates complete tasks as they try to outwit the Impostor. Check out what they are all about.

RAISE THE BAR

Every time a task is completed, the task bar at the top of the screen begins to fill up. Completing the task bar gives Crewmates a victory and there are a range of missions around each map to complete. Some tasks are easy, but others are more complex and require teamwork and strategy.

DEAD GOOD

Even if Crewmates are eliminated, they must still carry on doing their tasks to help their team. Other players won't see ghosts (dead Crew) in action and they can't communicate either. So, even if you're annoyed at leaving the game, don't give up and keep working to defeat the Impostor!

24

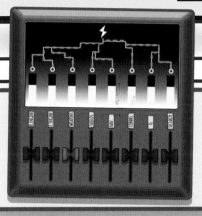

Task type: SHORT
These tasks are just a single simple step in one location and are the easiest to complete.

Task type: LONG
Tasks that need more than one step, often with the player having to wait or move to another part of the map.

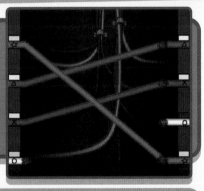

Task type: COMMON
Given to all of the Crewmates and required to be done by every Crew member. Can include card swipe, key insert and ID code.

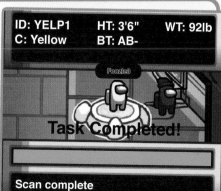

Task type: VISUAL
When being done, visual tasks give a display to others that the mission is actually in process. Clearing asteroids and emptying garbage are visual tasks.

10 TASK TIPS

Listen up, Crewmates! Take note of these ten task tips to help you survive and succeed in defeating the evil player among you...

Task tip 1

Don't forget the tasks you've done. When a meeting is called, remember what missions you have completed so you can tell the rest and begin to root out the lying Impostor.

Task tip 2

Think about doing long tasks first. There will then be more Crew around, which should stop the Impostor from killing you while you're busy, for fear of being seen in the awful act!

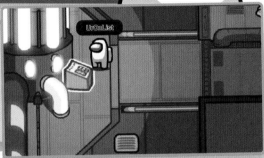

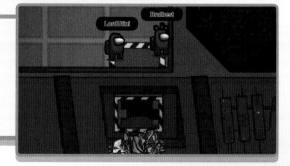

Task tip 3

Keep the Crew together. Doing any type of task by yourself can be dangerous – the Impostor could step in or appear through a vent and wipe you out.

Task tip 4

Do visual tasks while other Crewmates are watching. This is the perfect way to prove your innocence and get the team to support you in voting.

Task tip 5

In settings, keep the 'visual tasks on' option selected, especially if you're an inexperienced player. Switching it off makes it easier for the Impostor.

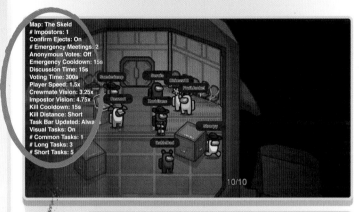

Map: The Skeld
Impostors: 1
Confirm Ejects: On
Emergency Meetings: 2
Anonymous Votes: Off
Emergency Cooldown: 15s
Discussion Time: 15s
Voting Time: 300s
Player Speed: 1.5x
Crewmate Vision: 3.25x
Impostor Vision: 4.75x
Kill Cooldown: 15s
Kill Distance: Short
Task Bar Updated: Alwa
Visual Tasks: On
Common Tasks: 1
Long Tasks: 3
Short Tasks: 5

10/10

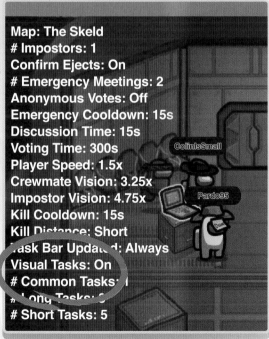

Map: The Skeld
Impostors: 1
Confirm Ejects: On
Emergency Meetings: 2
Anonymous Votes: Off
Emergency Cooldown: 15s
Discussion Time: 15s
Voting Time: 300s
Player Speed: 1.5x
Crewmate Vision: 3.25x
Impostor Vision: 4.75x
Kill Cooldown: 15s
Kill Distance: Short
Task Bar Updated: Always
Visual Tasks: On
Common Tasks:
Long Tasks:
Short Tasks: 5

27

Task tip 6

Some Crewmates like doing visual tasks around the mid point of a match, rather than straight away. Saving these tasks lets you prove your innocence if doubt begins to rise about you.

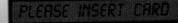

Task tip 7

If a task takes up the whole screen, a Crewmate won't be able to spot any incoming danger. Don't do these while you suspect an attack may be coming!

Task tip 8

Crucial sabotage task fixes, like the Reactor and O2, must be done or the Crew will die. If you arrive and see someone already fixing it, that's a good sign they are not the Impostor.

Task tip 9

Spotting a player standing or spending lots of time in a room that doesn't have many tasks could be a giveaway. Crewmates will usually be too busy to do this!

COUNTING ON YOU

There are nearly 40 different tasks to do around The Skeld, MIRA HQ and Polus. You'll always have lots of duties to carry out!

DESTROYED: 2

How come I always get the **worst** tasks?!

Task tip 10

Common tasks are given to every Crew member. If you spot a player doing a common task that you don't have, then they must be faking and are an Impostor!

29

TEAM UP

Crewmates' powers are greatly boosted by working together as a group. The Impostor will struggle against these clever tactics.

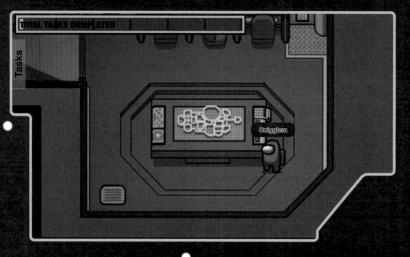

BREAK OUT

Spotting the Impostor in Among Us is very difficult without the full support of the Crew around you. Don't leap from one task straight to another – take a quick break to assess what's happening nearby and in other rooms. Look at how a player moves, whether they back away from a group or appear to act suspicious. Just staying focused on tasks could mean that your team of Crewmates misses a vital clue that gives the Impostor away!

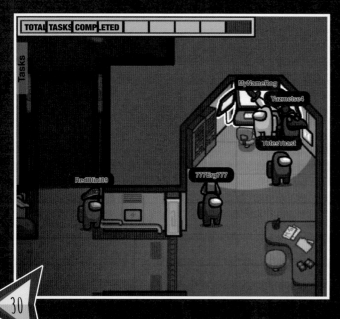

CLOSE THE GAP

If the task bar is almost full, a good tactic is to get the remaining Crewmates together and complete the rest of the tasks as a group. This makes life a misery for the Impostor or Impostors, as they can't pick off members without being spotted by the large gathering.

DOUBLE DELIGHT

If you spend a chunk of time pairing up with another Crewmate and, even when no other player is around, they don't kill you, then it's a good sign that the person is not the Impostor. Be sure to say this during discussions to help your team work out who is the nasty dude among you.

LIGHT THE WAY

During the lights out sabotage, unlike a regular Crewmate the Impostors can still see perfectly and will be able to navigate with ease. If you suspect that a player's actions and behaviour means they've still had perfect vision in the dark, let the Crew know your thoughts and build a case against that player.

I can't see a thing!

31

TEXT TALK

Discussing key game developments and saying who you suspect is the Impostor is crucial for the Crew!

The discussion, which happens after a body is reported or an emergency meeting is called, is a key time. Treat it very importantly and speak up. But, don't talk too much because it may make you look suspicious when actually you're an innocent Crewmate!

As a Crewmate, trust no-one and keep an open mind in the discussions. The Impostor among you will say all sorts to make them look safe!

Stay confident and communicate clearly. Always be precise when asked what you were doing and where you were in the match during discussions!

You may see players use certain words and phrases during discussions. Keep up to speed with in-game language and know what terms like 'sus' (suspicious) and 'elec' (Electrical room) really mean!

If you have absolute proof that you know the Impostor, such as seeing them kill or vent, say so at the very beginning of the discussion!

The group discussions may not always go your way. You may not have time to type what you want or the Impostor may succeed in framing you. Keep your cool and remember to learn from it and come back stronger in the next game!

33

MAKE YOUR VOTE

Every Crewmate vote counts, so make sure you know the strategies and secrets that arise as you make up your mind.

Don't be scared to hit the 'skip vote' button. If you can't trust what you're being told in discussion before the vote, then relax and see what plays out ahead of the next voting opportunity.

If a player votes very early, which is shown by the 'I voted' tag appearing, is this a sign they are actually the Impostor and trying to shift blame? Keep this theory in mind and watch how voting rolls out.

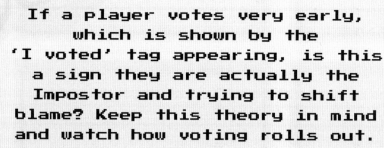

Keep an eye on the 'voting ends in' countdown and vote late, if you want to see how the rest of the Crew decides to go. Going with the majority vote may sometimes be a good strategy.

34

If you've buddied up with a player in the map and done tasks together, you may want to follow them in the vote stage too. Pay attention to what that player says in discussion.

GAME CHANGER

In a November 2020 update, 'anonymous voting' was added as a setting option. There's no way to see how your Crew voted with this on!

Once voting is over, you can see the players who voted against you as their mini coloured helmets will appear next to your name. If you fancy getting back at a player, then remember this detail.

CRUCIAL CREW TIPS

A quick-fire round-up of some extra hints to keep the Crew ahead of the Impostor!

AVOID VENTS

Try not to stand around vents for too long. There's no need to because Crewmates can't use them, and if you're seen it will deffo raise unnecessary suspicion.

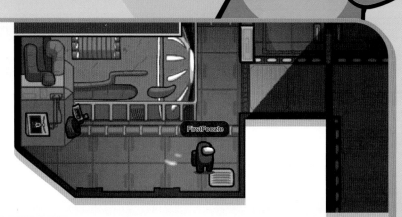

POWER UP

If you're a PC player, using the mouse and the keyboard and not just the mouse will make you a much more effective Crewmate. You'll move and respond more swiftly.

KNOW THE RISKS

Know each map's danger spots and approach them with extra care. For example, areas not covered by surveillance cameras, like Electrical room in The Skeld, are high risk and attract the Impostor's attention.

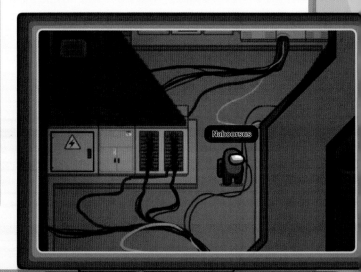

STAY CLOSE

Stay in a group of Crewmates, but don't get on top of each other too much. If Crew are huddled close together, the Impostor could strike and it's tough to detect who dealt it.

FIND THE ADMIN ROOM

Don't underestimate the importance of the Admin room and being able to see where Crewmates are. Always know how to reach this location for a helpful spy.

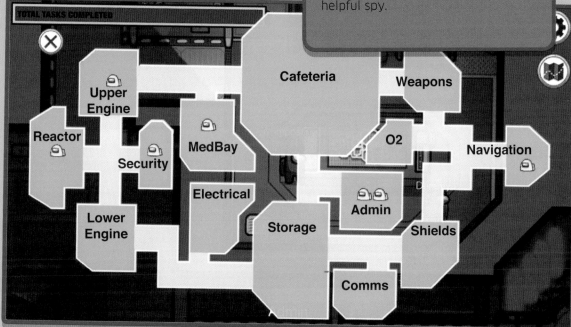

TOTAL TASKS COMPLETED

Upper Engine

Reactor

Security

MedBay

Cafeteria

Weapons

O2

Navigation

Electrical

Lower Engine

Storage

Admin

Shields

Comms

CHECK YOUR STATS

Okay, so this tip isn't crucial, but it's always good to look at your game statistics. You'll see stuff like the number of tasks completed, times ejected and Crewmate vote wins. You can work on boosting the stats that'll make you a winner!

Statistics

Bodies Reported:	149
Emergencies Called:	95
Tasks Completed:	1261
All Tasks Completed:	71
Sabotages Fixed:	236
Impostor Kills:	177
Times Murdered:	292
Times Ejected:	123
Crewmate Streak:	6
Times Impostor:	177
Times Crewmate:	856
Games Started:	1033
Games Finished:	704
Impostor Vote Wins:	38
Impostor Kill Wins:	52
Impostor Sabotage Wins:	5
Crewmate Vote Wins:	252
Crewmate Task Wins:	11

SPOT THE IMPOSTOR!

Time to start searching out the evil player among you.
It's a tough job, so pay attention!

KNOW THE SIGNS

Remember that the following behaviours and signs could give the
Impostor away at first glance. At the very least, they should make
a Crewmate aware that the person deserves a closer look...

**Moving with super
speed between
distant locations**
✔

**Quick to accuse
people in meetings**
✔

**Keen to get single
Crewmates on
their own**
✔

**Never seen
completing a
visual task**
✔

Appearing in random places

Likes to stay away from cameras

Lacking solid info and explanations when discussing

Either very loud or very quiet in the chats

FRIGHTENING FACT

Game developers InnerSloth say that the Impostor is actually an alien parasitic shapeshifter. Urgh!

HOW TO IDENTIFY IMPOSTORS

The next eight pages are packed with smart strategies and tips to help Crewmates identify the evil murdering folk!

REAL REPORT?

Self reporting is a trick the Impostor can try. It means they actually report a dead body after making the kill, because the Impostor believes the Crewmates won't think it's their doing. If you suspect a self report, call it out clearly in the chat and make the player fully explain their location and movements. Others may have further evidence to back up the sneaky self report that you detected!

QUICK ACTION

As soon as a report is made, all players have the chat feature and begin discussing. This gives the Impostor no time to hide in vents or close doors to make them look innocent.

DISCUSS!

DEAD BODY REPORTED

UPLOAD MISTAKE

Impostors will fake tasks to make them look like regular Crewmates. If a player starts the upload task in Admin at the very start of a game, then they are definitely not for real! This is because the upload can't be done until the download has been completed – at the immediate start of a match there isn't time to have the download done before the upload can be tackled. It's a fake move and needs to be identified by the Crew!

TOTAL TASKS COMPLETED

Sabotage and kill everyone.
Fake Tasks:
Electrical: Fix Wiring (0/3)
Admin: Swipe Card
Reactor: Start Reactor
Storage: Fuel Engines (0/2)
O2: Empty Chute (0/2)
Electrical: Divert Power to Shields (0/2)
Cafeteria: Download Data (0/2)
Shields: Prime Shields
Electrical Calibrate Distributor
Navigation: Chart Course

Tasks

10Wigform

ANYBODY ELSE GOT A SPLITTING HEADACHE?

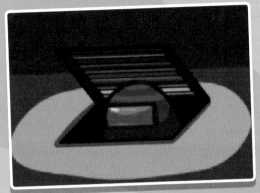

VANISHING VENT ACT

This seems like a super simple strategy, but it's amazing how many players don't know about this clever Crewmate move! Wait around to see a player enter a room, then stand by the entrance for five to ten seconds. When you enter, if the person has vanished through a vent, then you know for sure they are the Impostor! Doing this in the Electrical room on The Skeld is a wise choice, because it's a popular place to vent from.

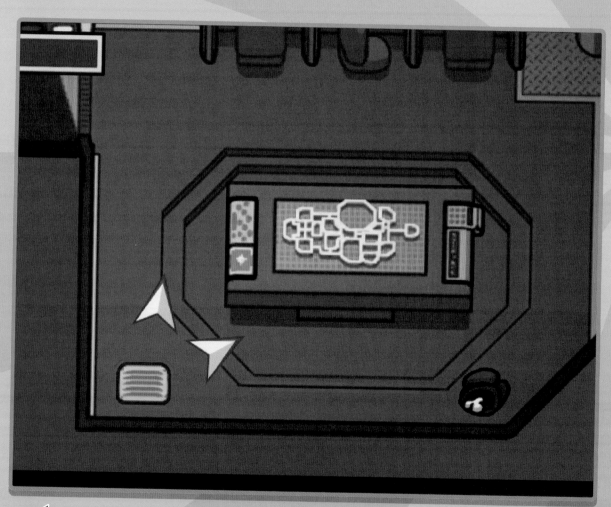

TRYING TOO HARD

In the discussion, using phrases like "trust me" and "not gonna lie" could be a sign that the Impostor is trying too hard to cover up their deed. An inexperienced Impostor could feel under pressure to reveal fake information, and chat away at length to make people believe them.

CleverTrevor
who is it?

PigHooey
trust me, it's black

FellBeast99
proof?

PigHooey
not gonna lie, black looks sus

GuyCognito
No way

0/100

NOT GONNA LIE – IT'S COLD OUT HERE!

UN-LOCKY!

When the Impostor is successfully ejected from The Skeld, they are flung through the ship's airlock into space. Bye bye, bad guy!

43

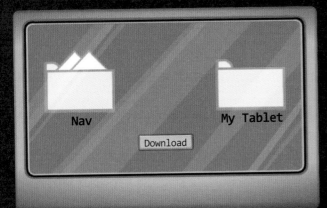

Nav

My Tablet

Download

TIME TRIALS

As well as knowing how to do the tasks and what tasks are in each room, Crewmates should also have a good idea of how long it takes to do them. For example, the 'start the reactor' task may take around 20 seconds, so if in a meeting a Crewmate claims they did it in just a few seconds and you have evidence they are lying, then question them about it. This takes practice, knowledge and the ability to remember what you've seen around the map.

MULTI TASKING

Remember what the tasks with multiple steps are, such as fuel engines in The Skeld. Crewmates will need to wait and move to new locations to finish it, and of course Impostors will only be able to fake this.

REFUEL STATION

LoneStarve

CLOSE KILLER

In many instances, the player first spotted nearest to the dead body is the evil Impostor among you. It seems a very basic detective technique, but often it's the right one. New players acting as the Impostor regularly fail to vent or escape the murder scene quickly, or don't have the confidence to self report. So trust your instinct and if you spot a player near to a body and it's not reported, then they are seriously sus!

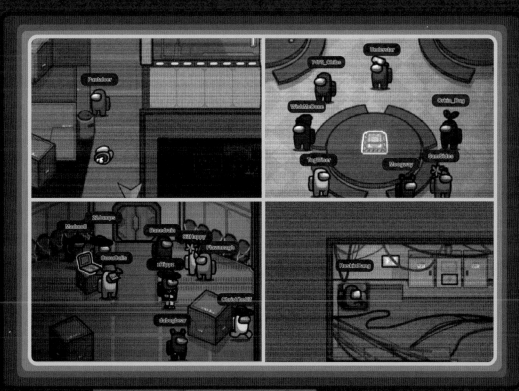

UN-BAR-LIEVABLE

Every Crewmate needs to know this Impostor identifying tip! When the rogue killer is pretending to do tasks and hanging around equipment for no reason, watch what happens the moment they step away. If it's a genuine task they have finished, the task bar will move up. If there's no movement in the bar, that person could be faking and is the Impostor in the game! This method is not totally foolproof though, as the bar may still move because another player finishes a task elsewhere at the same time.

TOTAL TASKS COMPLETED

Admin: Swipe Card
MedBay: Submit Scan
Weapons: Download Data (0/2)
Electrical: Divert Power to O2 (0/2)
Reactor Meltdown in 21 (1/2)

Tasks

UncleGyms

BOREDOM BUSTER

As a Crewmate, watch out for the Impostor showing signs of boredom and a lack of concentration. Genuine Crewmates are busy doing tasks around the map, but Impostors won't be and, for example, they may enter a room and appear to do nothing. If a player is standing still, crashing into walls or looking lost, it could be that they have nothing to do and are not focusing properly. These actions should make you question their real identity.

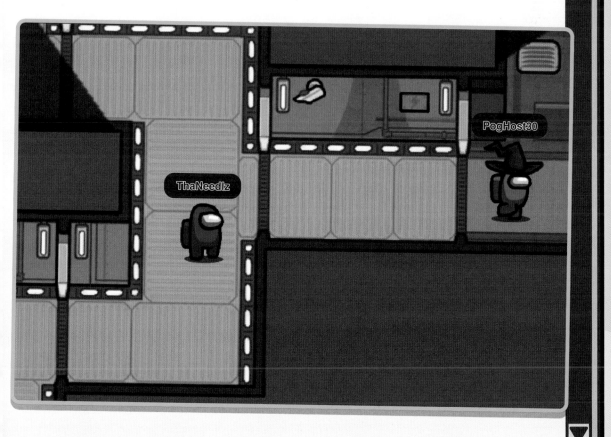

IMPOSTOR'S HANDBOOK

When you're selected to be the Impostor in Among Us, you need to act and think very differently to the rest of the Crewmates. Your job is to be sneaky, secretive and sly as you seek to slay players without raising suspicions. It's a tough task, but luckily you're about to uncover everything you need to be an awesome Impostor. Let the evil actions begin!

GOING IT ALONE

Are you brave enough to take on the Impostor's role?
Be strong and keep your cool while being cruel.

SOLO STYLE

Being the Impostor is a lonely mission. Sure, you spawn with the rest of the Crew, but from the moment a match starts, your objective is to get among the players and cause havoc. Killings and sabotages are your primary tools, and you can also lock players in and vent around the map for maximum chaos. You're on your own and no other player has your back...

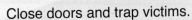

Close doors and trap victims.

DOUBLE TROUBLE

...apart from when there's more than one Impostor! You can also select to join a game that has two or three evil players. Do this if you want an extra dose of danger and more lethal lies in the discussion. New players should keep clear of multiple Impostor matches because it takes time to understand the tactics used. However, if you're chosen as the baddie and you know there's one or two more of you, at least you have a fiendish friend with you.

FREE PLAY

Just as when you're a normal Crewmate, use the free play sessions to get to grips with being the Impostor. Go to the laptop in the Cafeteria, and from the Task Tester 2000 select the red Impostor file to switch your role. These practice sessions will sharpen your skills while being the cruel character. There are limits to what you can do and the dummy players are not very smart, but it gives you a taste of venting, killing and more.

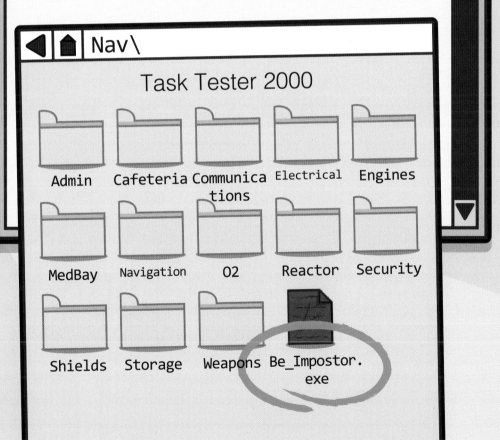

Nav \

Task Tester 2000

Admin	Cafeteria	Communications	Electrical	Engines
MedBay	Navigation	O2	Reactor	Security
Shields	Storage	Weapons	Be_Impostor.exe	

CROWD CONTROL

As the Impostor, it's absolutely vital to blend in with the Crew and look like a regular player.

ACT INNOCENT

From the start, try to think just like you would as a Crewmate. Move around with urgency, appear busy and don't look ultra sus by doing nothing and appearing to have no strategy. Don't keep switching your direction, as you may look like you're trying to track down a solo player for a kill. You need a split personality – think and act like both a Crewmate and Impostor at once!

ACCURATE AGGRESSION

Don't appear too weak or too strong, especially when texting during meetings. Being loud and a bit aggressive in discussions could make you stand out from the crowd, which is not what you want. Equally, fading into the background and keeping quiet is not wise either – players will certainly think you have something to hide.

| Color | Hat | Pet | Skin | Game |

STUDY SETTINGS

When you set your appearance, always check what settings the host has chosen. Knowing the kill cooldown time is crucial. Keep an eye on Crewmate vision and Impostor vision, task bar updates and kill distance too. These impact on your abilities and what you can expect as the killer.

Nasty numbers

Remember that if the number of Impostors remaining on the map is the same as the number of Crewmates, it's a victory for evil. That's a bonus of playing a baddie with one or two more Impostors also present.

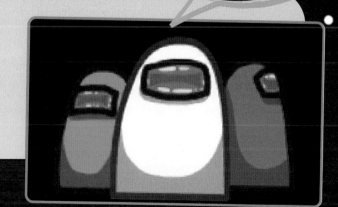

I love you guys!

5 FAKE TASK TIPS

When it comes to doing pretend tasks around the map, these five tips will help the Impostor fool the Crewmates!

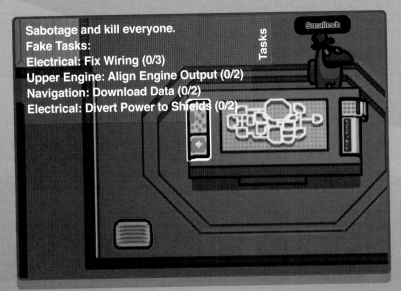

Sabotage and kill everyone.
Fake Tasks:
Electrical: Fix Wiring (0/3)
Upper Engine: Align Engine Output (0/2)
Navigation: Download Data (0/2)
Electrical: Divert Power to Shields (0/2)

Tasks

Smallech

PRETEND PLAY

To make you appear innocent, the Impostor is always given a list of fake tasks to do. You can't actually do the missions required, but check the list carefully and only pretend to do these tasks that are listed. Stand and move just as you would while doing the genuine job, which requires knowledge of what's involved for each one and how long they should take.

Fake task tip 1

Know which fake tasks are the better ones to do and won't cause heaps of suspicion and strange looks from Crewmates. For example, on The Skeld there are five spots where you can possibly be told to do the 'download data' task, which include Cafeteria, Weapons and Navigation rooms. For fix wiring there are six possible locations. Some of these are in very visible places, like outside Security, so make sure you fake these jobs very precisely just in case you are watched.

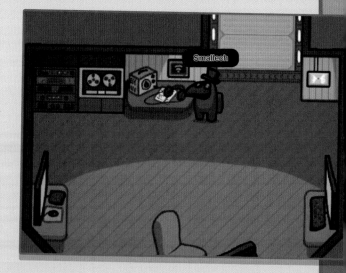

Smallech

Fake task tip 2

Sometimes the game host may set visual tasks to 'off', which is a great bonus for the Impostor. It means you can't be called out for doing a visual task, such as 'clear asteroids' on The Skeld, and the on-screen indicators for tasks like these won't appear. Being caught faking a visual task is evidence for the Crewmates that you're the one to vote off!

Color	Hat	Pet	Skin	Game

Crewmate Vision	− 1.75x +
Impostor Vision	− 1.75x +
Kill Cooldown	− 10.0s +
Kill Distance	− Long +
Visual Tasks	☐
Task Bar Updates	− Always +
# Common Tasks	− 0 +

Fake task tip 3

You should understand that the 'prime shields task', in the Shields room on The Skeld, is a visual one. Lots of players don't know this. The second time the task's set off in a game, it will still appear brightly. Stay clear of this tricky mission as it's so easy to be spotted as a faker if the Crewmates have a basic knowledge of how 'prime shields' operates.

NobooRug

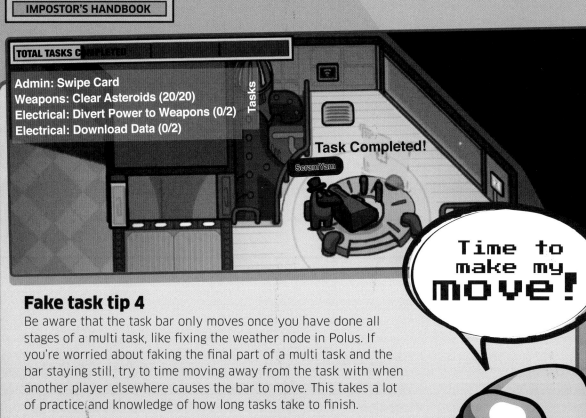

TOTAL TASKS COMPLETED

Admin: Swipe Card
Weapons: Clear Asteroids (20/20)
Electrical: Divert Power to Weapons (0/2)
Electrical: Download Data (0/2)

Tasks

Task Completed!

ScramYam

Time to make my **move!**

Fake task tip 4

Be aware that the task bar only moves once you have done all stages of a multi task, like fixing the weather node in Polus. If you're worried about faking the final part of a multi task and the bar staying still, try to time moving away from the task with when another player elsewhere causes the bar to move. This takes a lot of practice and knowledge of how long tasks take to finish.

POPULAR TASK TIMES

Empty garbage	(The Skeld)	5 secs (part 1) 6 secs (part 2)
Clean O2 filter	(The Skeld)	6 secs
Prime shields	(The Skeld)	2 secs
Align telescope	(Polus)	5 secs
Measure weather	(MIRA HQ)	5 secs
Buy beverage	(MIRA HQ)	7 secs

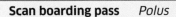

Fake task tip 5

This is a super simple rule to follow – ignore this and you'll be the easiest Impostor to spot in the history of Among Us! Common tasks must be done by all players in the game. Never fake a common task that nobody has been given in your match. Even if one player spots you, it's enough evidence for them to spread in a meeting. Look closely at what the commons are and don't pretend to enter the ID code on MIRA HQ, for example, if there's no need!

COMMON TASKS

Fix wiring	*The Skeld, MIRA HQ, Polus*
Enter ID code	*MIRA HQ*
Insert keys	*Polus*
Swipe card	*The Skeld, Polus*
Scan boarding pass	*Polus*

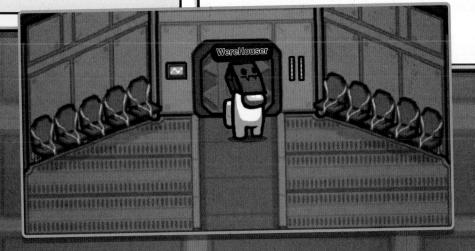

57

DEADLY DETAILS!

The Impostor must be a cool, clever and ruthless killer.
These deadly details reveal how to wipe out Crewmates in
a wicked way.

EARLY ADVANCE

Get safe and easy kills early on. Yes, there are
more potential witnesses, but an Impostor should
always take the chance to destroy a player if
no-one sees it and you're not on cameras. There
are plenty of players to blame in a meeting, too.
Check the kill distance setting of your game.
At 'long', you can murder from a good distance
away but at 'short' you'll need sneaky tactics and
confidence to strike close up.

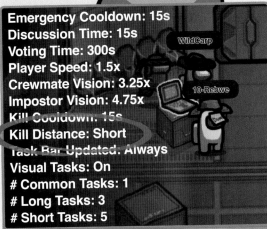

Emergency Cooldown: 15s
Discussion Time: 15s
Voting Time: 300s
Player Speed: 1.5x
Crewmate Vision: 3.25x
Impostor Vision: 4.75x
Kill Cooldown: 15s
Kill Distance: Short
Task Bar Updated: Always
Visual Tasks: On
Common Tasks: 1
Long Tasks: 3
Short Tasks: 5

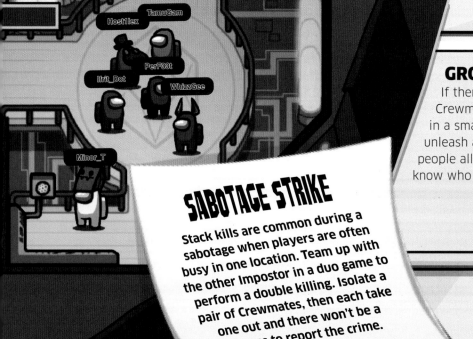

GROUP STRIKE

If there are four or more
Crewmates on top of each other
in a small space, join them to
unleash a stack kill. With so many
people all together, the Crew won't
know who did the deed.

SABOTAGE STRIKE

Stack kills are common during a
sabotage when players are often
busy in one location. Team up with
the other Impostor in a duo game to
perform a double killing. Isolate a
pair of Crewmates, then each take
one out and there won't be a
witness to report the crime.
Slick stuff!

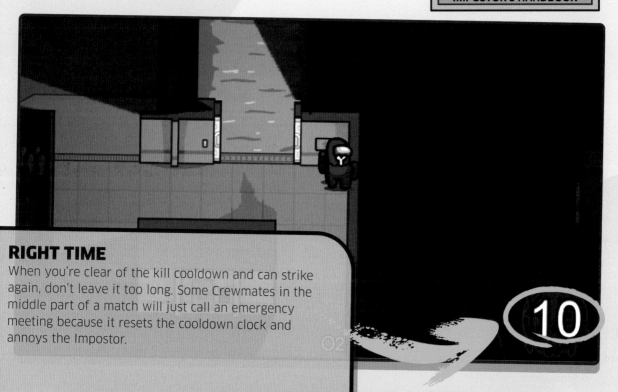

RIGHT TIME

When you're clear of the kill cooldown and can strike again, don't leave it too long. Some Crewmates in the middle part of a match will just call an emergency meeting because it resets the cooldown clock and annoys the Impostor.

INNOCENT TARGET

A Crewmate who has proved their innocence to others, such as being seen doing a visual task, is a top target to kill. Players will trust and listen to them, so an Impostor needs to make that player disappear!

GOING UNDERGROUND

Only Impostors can use the vents. They are very useful, but also come with some warning signs.

HIDE INSIDE

Impostors can effectively hide in vents and wait to kill a lone Crewmate who enters the room. Then, going back into the underground tunnel and waiting for a player to report the body takes the game straight to the discussion, with no-one seeing the Impostor's movements.

LOCKDOWN

The Impostor will try to lock doors to a room and kill the trapped person, obviously making sure that no other player has spotted the move. Jumping in a vent to escape the scene to another room is usually a tempting tactic to take! Impostors could also close the door in an empty room before venting away as extra security against being seen.

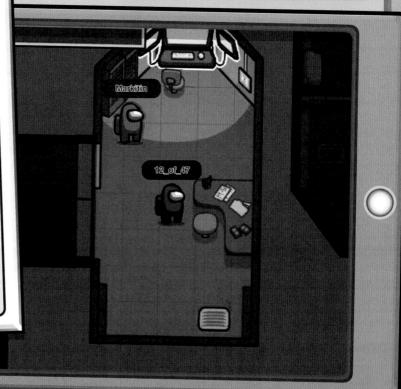

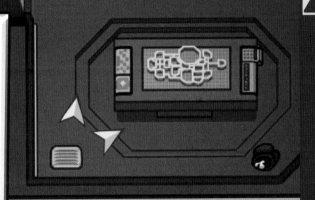

TIME TUNNEL

Be aware that when you dive down a vent as the Impostor, if the kill cooldown is in action it will be paused. So Impostors can't hide down there for too long, because they need to be out in the open for the time to tick down until a kill can be possible again.

REMEMBER ROOMS

Not every room has a vent, so remember which locations do have one in case you plan to make a kill and then want to leave quickly through the floor. In MIRA HQ, the Communications and Storage don't have vents for the Impostors to sneak through.

SCREEN SAVER

Want to be extra clever? While a Crewmate's doing a task that you know will take up most of their screen, you can creep in, kill them and then exit through the vent so no-one nearby connects you to the body.

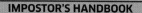

SABOTAGE: THE SKELD

The are five types of sabotage: communications, doors, lights, O2 and reactor. Use this map to find out how to use them!

When doors are locked, all other sabotages can't be used until the door lock countdown resets.

Upper Engine

Reactor

Security

MedBay

Comms sabotage also disables the cameras in Security, giving the Impostor a chance to kill without being seen.

Electrical

Lower Engine

Storage

When you're inside with a lone Crewmate, lock the doors to electrical in The Skeld and make a cool kill.

Only one major sabotage can be used at once and there's a cooldown time.

Use communications sabotage to knock out the map in the Admin area.

Weapons

Cafeteria

O2

Navigation

Admin

Click the sabotage icon in the bottom right of the main screen, then press the circular sabotage button that you want to set off.

Shields

Communications

Flick the communications sabotage and Crewmates won't know where to go to do their tasks.

63

SABOTAGE: MIRA HQ

Take a trip to company headquarters for another stack
of sabotages and master moves to defeat the Crewmates!

**MIRA HQ is not so full of sabotage
opportunities as The Skeld. There are no
door lock options here for Impostors to use.**

Set off the reactor to get the Crewmates racing to
the left side to fix it. Lost players on the right of the
map can become the Impostor's victims!

Reactor

Decontamination

O2 sabotage is an
option in MIRA
HQ and The Skeld.
On this map, a
code must be
entered in two
places before
the lethal timer
expires.

Launchpad

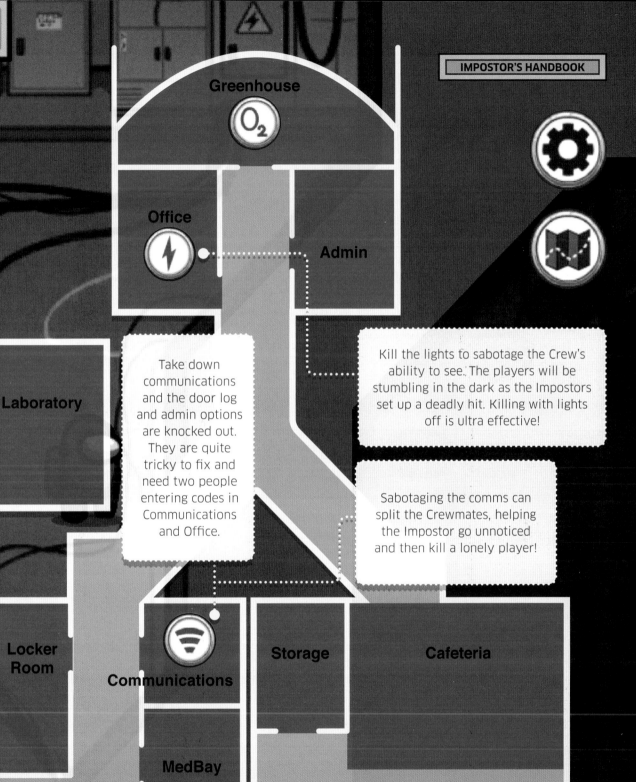

Greenhouse

O₂

Office

Admin

Laboratory

Take down communications and the door log and admin options are knocked out. They are quite tricky to fix and need two people entering codes in Communications and Office.

Kill the lights to sabotage the Crew's ability to see. The players will be stumbling in the dark as the Impostors set up a deadly hit. Killing with lights off is ultra effective!

Sabotaging the comms can split the Crewmates, helping the Impostor go unnoticed and then kill a lonely player!

Locker Room

Communications

Storage

Cafeteria

MedBay

Balcony

SABOTAGE: POLUS

Understand the sabotage scene around this large and cold location. There are plenty of places for Impostors to do damage.

Dropship

Crewmates rush over here to fix the lights and stop the deadly darkness. An Impostor can use the vent in the top left area to escape after a sneaky solo kill.

Like The Skeld, door sabotages are in action and can trap and confuse players in Polus, especially those new to this map.

Electrical

Security

Comms are fixed at the pylon in the centre, so Impostors will be aware of heavy traffic there when this fix is needed.

Door sabotages can still be used while other sabotages are in operation. This is an extra tactical tool for Impostors.

O2

Communications

Disabling comms will wipe out admin map, vitals monitor and cameras.

Weapons

The reactor sabotage is called the seismic stabilizers on Polus.

Unique to Polus is that doors have to be opened by Crew doing a small task, rather than being locked in for the standard ten seconds by the Impostor.

Laboratory

Storage

Polus is a large map and in the mid and late game, quiet areas are great spots for a quick Impostor kill.

Office

Specimen Room

Admin

TALKING A GOOD GAME

Get your chat and text responses ready for the discussion. As the Impostor, you always need to 'talk a good game' and keep suspicion away.

If a Crewmate questions you in the discussion, reveal the 'tasks' you have done and be specific. Mention your mission and the room you were in — it may help shift the blame away from you.

If you are spotted making a kill or using a vent, try to accuse and question that witness straight away in the meeting. Getting your argument in first could keep the heat off you, especially in a game that has a quick discussion time setting.

Make friends early on. If you can back up a Crewmate and say you saw them doing a task, for example, you could win allies and the support of the group. Suckers!

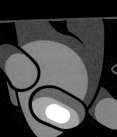

If you double bluff and call an emergency meeting or you self-report a body, make your point and try to control the talk. Don't hit the button and then have nothing convincing to say!

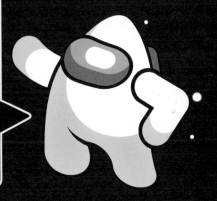

Remember which players vote against you. See the player icons that may appear by your name in the voting stage and get ready to target those players later on.

When the discussion looks like it may head to a skip vote call, then go along with it as well. A skip vote won't do you any harm and gives you another round to kill off weak Crewmates!

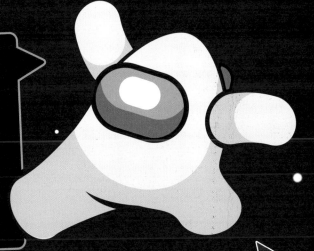

ADVANCED TACTICS

Scan the following eight pages to pick up pro tactics and tips to take your Impostor game to the next level.

VICIOUS VENTING

Being caught using the vents is bad news when you're the Impostor. Chances are that the eagle-eyed Crewmate will then race to the emergency meeting button to call a discussion and spill the beans about you. But if you move quickly and vent to the Cafeteria, where The Skeld's emergency button is, you can head the player off and kill them before they get the chance to do it. You need super speed and good knowledge of where vents lead to, but it can be done!

HALLWAY HORROR

On the MIRA HQ map, make use of the decontamination hallway near to the Reactor, on the left central side of the map. When entered, both doors will lock and whoever is inside becomes trapped. This is an ideal situation for the Impostor, who can make an easy kill and then jump through the area's vent to escape the scene. New Crewmates may not be aware of this and an evil Impostor should be looking to make decontamination a deadly place.

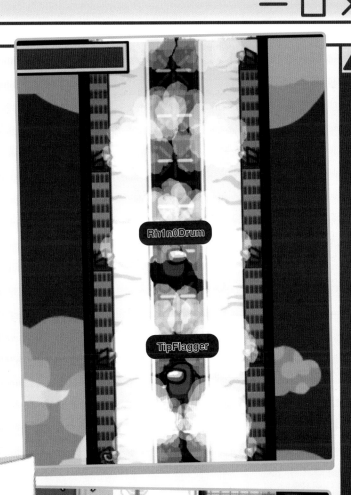

DOUBLE DECONTAMINATION

On Polus, there are two decontamination rooms for the Impostor to focus on for killings. They are both in corridors that come off the Specimen room, in the bottom right of the map.

RETURN TO THE SCENE

How about this for a cheeky, but clever, killer's move! After you have knocked a body, vent away and then team up with a random Crewmate. Try to lead this person back to the room the body is in and you'll discover the death together. The Crewmate you're with will confirm your alibi during the discussion, making you look like an innocent dude. It's sooo smart, but needs plenty of nerve to carry off.

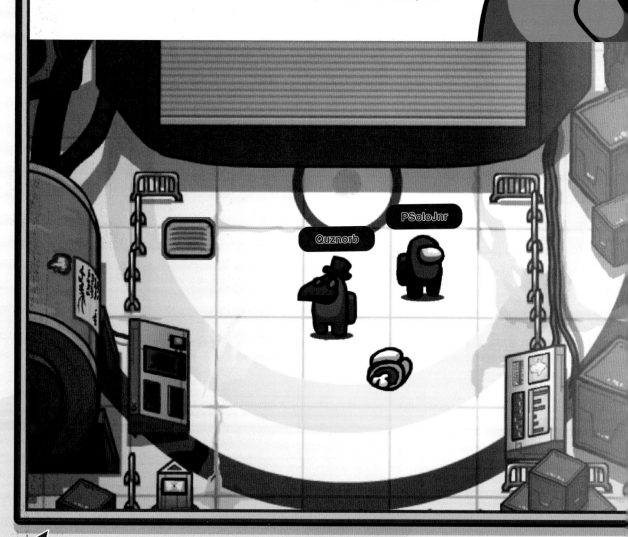

WRONG MOVE

The pressure is really on during the discussion and vote. The Impostor needs to say all the right things to convince, however the Crewmates can often give you some help along the way. If another player is wrongly accused, quickly jump on it and back up the false claim. If there are other Impostors playing too, a tactic is to team up and make sure the accused gets the boot. Always read closely what the Crew are typing about..

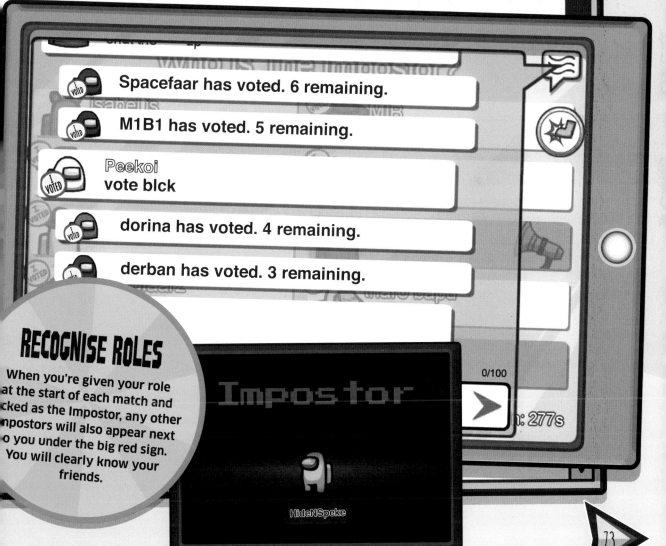

Spacefaar has voted. 6 remaining.

M1B1 has voted. 5 remaining.

Peekoi
vote blck

dorina has voted. 4 remaining.

derban has voted. 3 remaining.

0/100

Impostor

n: 277s

HideNSpeke

RECOGNISE ROLES

When you're given your role at the start of each match and cked as the Impostor, any other mpostors will also appear next o you under the big red sign. You will clearly know your friends.

SABOTAGE SWITCH

Sabotages are a crucial weapon for the Impostor, as they give Crewmates a task and distraction from what the evil player may be up to. At times, though, the Impostor may want to be seen actually fixing their sabotage! This could seem strange and not help get a victory, but it gives the Crewmates a reason not to suspect the Impostor as they have been eyeballed doing a critical task for the team. Use this move at times to create some trust during voting.

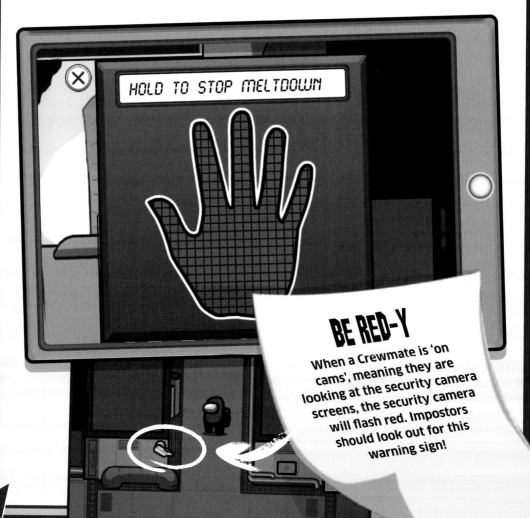

HOLD TO STOP MELTDOWN

BE RED-Y

When a Crewmate is 'on cams', meaning they are looking at the security camera screens, the security camera will flash red. Impostors should look out for this warning sign!

SCREEN TIME

Not getting caught on cameras in The Skeld and Polus is an important rule for Impostors. These cameras can be used to the killer's benefit as well, though! In The Skeld's Security room, the cameras show four hallway locations, including right outside Security. If you see a lone player on the screen in this hallway, you can head straight there and make a kill. CCTV can be a valuable tool at times!

MULTI MADNESS

This is a killing method for high level Impostors, but learn to perfect this strategy and you'll rack up some quality takedowns! Known as the vent multi-kill move, you should start by hiding inside a room's vent and wait for a Crewmate to appear. Then, make a quick surprise kill, hit the sabotage button and hide out in the room while cooldown is in action. Then vent again and when a new player appears in the room, kill that person before they can report the dead body. It's a deadly series of actions!

STRIKE EARLY

Vent multi-kills are best done early on. Don't use it too often because when you don't appear to help with sabotages, the Crew will become suspicious.

TOTAL TASKS COMPLETED

Sabotage and Kill everyone.
Fake Tasks:
Office: Swipe Card
O2: Downlaod Data (0/2)
Laboratory: Repair Drill
Specimen Room: Store Artifacts

Tasks

FastFate88

FOOL AROUND

For a cheeky Impostor tip that probably won't win you many friends, it can often be a sly strategy to pretend you're a new player. Wandering around without a clue in the match and saying you don't understand certain things in the chat may get you some sympathy among the Crewmates when you're the Impostor. Clever players could work you out pretty soon, but claiming you're a noob and even making it look like you're AFK (away from keyboard) at times should be an occasional option to use. Good luck fooling the best Among Us folk!

Please
help,
I am new!
(Honest!)

IMPOSTOR'S CHECKLIST

You've discovered all the best tips and sneaky moves to make you a top Impostor in Among Us. Here's a quick rundown of the essentials you need to know...

Know which tasks to fake and avoid visual missions ✔

Fake tasks and move when the task bar rises ✔

Victory

KrBlooey

DapperDanv

Carry out stack kills to disguise your Impostor role ✔

78

Kill off weak Crewmates early to cause disruption in the discussions

✔

Develop a calm lying technique and be quick to accuse during chats with Crewmates

✔

Team up with the other Impostors for double kills and targeting Crewmates

✔

Understand when to vent and how to escape and enter rooms for maximum damage

✔

Unleash sabotages at the right time in the right place to panic the map

✔

Stay off cams in The Skeld and Polus when killing and lie about what you've seen on MIRA HQ's doorlog

✔

NOTES

Crew mate

Impostor